Want to know

Why They Are

RICH

& You Are Not?

Here's your chance to learn the secrets of the Rich

By
Ansel Clarke

ISBN (PB): 979-8-89604-005-7

ISBN (HB): 979-8-89604-006-4

Published by: Writer Cosmos

Credits
Editor: Frank Williams
Cover Design: Lisa Smith
Layout & Design: Raymond Reynolds

Dedication

To my wife Jacki and my kids Addi and Alex, whose love and support inspire me to be a better man each day. And to all the dreamers—may you find something in my story that will encourage and inspire you to dream, make better choices, ask better questions, and chase your dreams of financial freedom and happiness.

About the Author

Ansel is a deeply private person who derives immense satisfaction from witnessing others achieve their goals and succeed. He believes that accumulating wealth should not be a competitive endeavor, nor should financial literacy be exclusive to the affluent. His foremost aspiration is to assist and inspire others. With this in mind, he has authored this short book, hoping that its contents will resonate with someone, motivating them to transform their narrative and positively impact the lives of their children and loved ones.

Acknowledgment

I want to express my deepest gratitude to Jacki, Terry, my beautiful niece Geneva, and everyone who supported and inspired me throughout this journey. To my editor for their invaluable feedback and patience; to my family, Jacki, Addi, and Alex, you are my ongoing inspiration. A special thanks to those who inspired the content of this book: Aunty P, SW, Charlie, and Sister Lawrence! Your stories shaped this work, and I am forever grateful.

Lastly, to my readers—thank you for taking the time to invest in your financial education. I hope this book serves as a valuable resource for your financial growth and responsibility. Let's choose to enrich each other and be that rising tide that lifts all boats on the journey to financial freedom.

Table of Contents

INTRODUCTION

Are you tired of being the poor, broke friend? Today, I will share with you some valuable insights into the mindset and experiences of the wealthy. I will recount my personal journey and motivations, highlighting the importance of my own narrative. Growing up in one of Jamaica's most impoverished neighborhoods, my mother struggled as a humble shopkeeper, while my father's absence left many questions unanswered. Tragedy struck when my mother passed away when I was just eleven years old, and I was subsequently sent to live with my aunt, whose household resembled a modern-day Cinderella story. As I resided with her and her three children, I found myself playing second fiddle, burdened with household chores, such as cleaning, dishwashing, and manual laundry. It was during this period that I recognized my desire for something greater.

As a teenager in my new 'family,' trivial arguments and reprimands over bread consumption and bathroom tissue usage often stemmed from a lack of financial resources. There were many days while at Kingston College when I had to really focus on hearing the day's lesson above my rumbling stomach. Determined to break this cycle, I vowed never to subject any future family of mine to such hardships. This realization fueled my aspiration for wealth. I admit without shame that I yearned for financial prosperity.

Over the next three decades, I embarked on a relentless quest for answers, diligently studying and seeking advice to understand why certain individuals achieved wealth while my family and I struggled financially. Through my exploration, I discovered that the key to wealth was not determined by the schools one attended, nationality, inherited wealth, or income level. Instead, I uncovered a fundamental truth: it is not about how much money one earns, but how good your financial IQ is, and how effectively you can convert your earned income into passive income, creating real wealth. I am eager to share these secrets, among others, to guide you towards your desired financial success.

After enduring seven challenging years with my aunt, a significant turning point arrived on Christmas Day when I was made homeless. I was taken in by a very kind family to whom I'm eternally grateful. However, this tale warrants its own dedicated platform, which we will explore in another context. Fast forward one year, three months, and four days, I found myself in a place called Negril in Jamaica, where I had the privilege of working alongside a remarkable individual who we will call SW. SW became my mentor and guardian of financial wisdom, not by his choice.

In an unplanned stroke of fate, his son also became my closest friend. I approached SW one day, humbly requesting his guidance on how to attain wealth. With a smile, he assessed the sincerity in my eyes, knowing I lacked the means to compensate him for his mentorship. In a light-hearted exchange, I offered to teach him how to enjoy life if he would impart his knowledge on wealth creation to me. Unbeknownst to me at the time, SW had already experienced a life filled with joy and abundance disguised in a cloak of humility. At least, that's how I saw it. He graciously took me under his wing for the next seven years, providing me with invaluable lessons that were not always easy to learn.

Allow me to share one of my cherished memories from this period. On one occasion, I approached SW regarding a malfunctioning swimming pool pump at his hotel, suggesting we call technicians to rectify the issue. To my surprise, he responded, "No, you will fix it," and he is not the kind of man you say no to. He entrusted me with the responsibility of fixing the swimming pool pump by handing me the manual. For the following three days, I diligently worked beneath the pool, striving to repair the pump. Although uncertain of the lesson SW intended to teach me, I persisted. Finally, with a sense of accomplishment and pride, I approached him with a wide grin, announcing that the pump was now functioning flawlessly. In response, he posed a simple question, "How do you feel?"

To this day, I struggle to express the overwhelming satisfaction and fulfillment I experienced in that moment. The lesson I took away from that experience was that it's never as difficult as you think it is if you have a manual to follow.

During my early twenties, I had the pleasure of meeting an extraordinary woman who has remained my devoted wife for the past three decades. She stood by my side despite my financial struggles, facing her own financial hardships. She saw something in me that many others failed to recognize. After initially dismissing me on our first encounter, claiming that I was bothersome, we found ourselves crossing paths again a few days later. It didn't take long for us to realize that there was a connection between us, and within two weeks of our first meeting, we decided to move in together. We were young, in love, physically fit, and financially challenged.

Our primary objective at that time was to save $10,000 Jamaican dollars, roughly equivalent to $65 USD. We inscribed this goal on a piece of paper and affixed it to the inside of the entry door to our rented room. Our living quarters were provided by a kind lady who operated an affordable rental establishment under the name of Brown Sugar. The significance behind the name eluded us, but we didn't dwell on it. Like any aspiring achievers, we understood the importance of documenting our goal and ensuring its feasibility. For us, it meant saving $10,000 JMD within a year, based on our combined salaries.

To achieve this objective, we were determined to overcome our negative financial situation and strive towards reaching a balance of zero. This meant settling all outstanding debts. Our first priority was to clear my wife's credit card bill, followed by the expenses accumulated at the local pub and restaurant. We express our gratitude to Susan and Jen for their assistance. The next significant financial burden was the substantial bill associated with my PADI (Professional Association of Diving Instructors) diving instructor qualification. However, with time and effort, we successfully eliminated all debts, including those from credit cards, banks, restaurants, and professional education. We celebrated the joyous moment of becoming debt-free. The weight of our past financial obligations had finally been lifted.

As we embarked on a new journey, we sought the path to financial freedom. However, I couldn't help but wonder what our next steps should be after clearing our debts.

Change Your Vocabulary – Change Your Reality!

I noticed that the more knowledge I gained about money, the more my vocabulary changed, and the more my financial situation improved. Could there really be a correlation? So, I decided to test this theory, convinced it couldn't be as simple as it seemed. Thus, my journey to enhance my financial intelligence commenced.

In the world I was accustomed to, one worked until the day they "checked out" of this life. That's just how life was supposed to be. Therefore, you can imagine my astonishment when my young and beautiful wife returned home one day from her job at a beach hotel, excitedly sharing her encounter with a delightful lady we shall refer to as Miss R here.

To my surprise, my wife revealed that this lady had retired at the age of 35. Retired? I questioned in disbelief. Wasn't retirement something only older individuals could consider? How was it possible for her to retire so young? What did she do for a living? And how could she afford to go on vacations? In my attempt to comprehend the enigma of this 35-year-old retiree, my mind delved into the search for answers. The answer lay in "passive income."

What on earth was passive income? In my understanding, income was earned through laboring for an employer. That's how everyone made their money - through hard work. At least, that's what I believed.

As my financial intelligence expanded, driven by my curiosity and the desire to ask better questions, I discovered a whole new world filled with unfamiliar terminologies and their meanings. As I grasped the significance behind these words, my vocabulary transformed from that of a working class individual to that of someone aspiring to attain financial freedom. This transformation opened up a new reality on the horizon. Words possess immense power. If you desire to alter your reality, embark on this journey of self-discovery.

My Relationship With Money

Only a couple of my dearest friends know what I'm about to make public. I hate money! I don't like touching it, counting it, or smelling it, but most of all, I really don't like what it does to people. I've witnessed firsthand that marriages often come undone because of money. We've all witnessed family feuds for what the "dead left," as we say. Brothers against brothers, sisters against sisters, and aunts and uncles getting into the mix for the money. Rich and poor alike are affected by this madness brought on by money, or should I say, a lack of it!

The world we live in is driven by economics, and we can't get away from it. So, what is one to do? How do I deal with not liking money but still fully understanding that I can't do without it? I decided to have more than I needed so I wouldn't have to think about it all the time. Now, I'm not telling you to be irresponsible and not keep a budget or have a financial statement for your household, but quite the opposite. If you do the right thing with money, you should have more than enough of it, as money is a reward for doing the right thing.

However, a word of caution is in order. Money should serve as a faithful servant, not a tyrannical master.

This brings me to the realization that the pursuit of wealth is not a competitive endeavor. Instead, it should resemble a rising tide that lifts all boats, benefiting not only an individual but also their family, friends, and colleagues. My perspective on money has evolved over time, and I now perceive it as a reward for doing the right things. What do I mean by that? Well, consider this: if I can serve more people better and at a more reasonable price, what do you think will transpire? Similarly, if you establish a reputation for providing exceptional customer service in your chosen field, what do you anticipate happening to your customer base? And if you treat your team not just fairly but with utmost respect and consideration, what outcome do you envision?

I deliberately refrain from providing direct answers to these questions, as one of the fundamental aspects of wealth-building lies in the ability to ask better questions. Allow me to reiterate – the ability to pose insightful queries is a pivotal ingredient in the journey towards prosperity.

I have a friend who frequently enquires about my wealth, asking if I am a millionaire or enquiring about my net worth. Needless to say, such inquiries make me exceedingly uncomfortable. However, what if there were better questions he could ask? For instance, he could enquire about how I transitioned from homelessness to the life I currently lead. He could ask about the steps I took to transform my circumstances.

Moreover, he could ponder whether the actions one takes hold more significance than the manner in which they are executed. These are all examples of more thought-provoking inquiries he could make. By asking better questions, one opens the door to receiving better answers. And thus, the lesson is learned – a key aspect of building wealth lies in the ability to ask insightful questions.

As alluded to earlier, here is your manual!

STEP 1
FIND A MENTOR

It is crucial to find a mentor for yourself as they are typically busy individuals. If you are eager to learn, they will teach you. However, if you are unwilling to learn, they will make it clear that their time should not be wasted. I recall a time when I went to my best friend and complained about his father. He had several sons, and those present looked at me with smiles, stating that I must be part of the family because that is precisely how their father treats them. SW played a significant role in my life as my mentor. He continues to be one of my all-time favorite people to this day. Whenever I face challenges that I cannot handle, I remind myself of the advice I received under his watch so many years ago. His wise words of wisdom have saved me from trouble, heartache, and financial difficulties. Thank you, SW!

So, what is the next step after deciding to become a wealthy individual? First, establish measurable goals. Set small, achievable goals instead of making vague statements like "I want to be rich" or "I want to have a lot of money." Define what "rich" means to you. For example, aim to save $10,000 in your bank account for investment within six months or a year, with a target date of December 21. Make your goals measurable and break them down into one-year goals that contribute to a larger five-year goal. It allows for a seamless progression from one goal to the next. Keep in mind that setting goals may change how your friends and associates perceive you. This is because you are focused on accumulating funds for investment while they may prioritize material possessions like luxury handbags, trendy boots, or partying.

Many people want rewards without putting in the necessary work. Over time, they may realize how much time and money they have wasted on fleeting items that lose value quickly. Be prepared to exercise discipline when your friends invite you out. Say no when necessary and stay committed to your goals. It is worth it! In other words, do not follow the crowd. If everyone is doing one thing, maybe you should consider doing the opposite, as it may increase your chances of success. For instance, if everyone is pissing their money up on a wall, maybe you should be saving yours! It's like if everyone is buying houses, it may be wise to sell yours, and when everyone is selling, it may be a good time to buy. Go against the crowd's actions.

Notes

STEP 2
FINANCIAL EDUCATION

Educating oneself is of utmost importance, particularly regarding financial education. There are three types of education that we should prioritize.

1. **<u>Academic Education</u>** – which encompasses subjects such as reading and writing and is typically obtained through high school and college.

2. **<u>Professional Education</u>** – which varies depending on individual career paths. For instance, one may start as a diving instructor, while others pursue professions like law, medicine, or engineering. However, for most people, education stops at this level. This leads us to the third type of education.

3. **<u>Financial Education</u>** – While schools may teach subjects like sex education or driving, financial education, which is far more important, is often neglected. This prompts the question: why aren't we taught about managing money, regardless of our social status, nationality or economic background, age or religious background? We all use money. As a self-professed conspiracy theorist, I wonder if this omission is intentional or merely coincidental. Allow me to share my opinion on this matter.

Although it is my personal belief, I consider it a factual observation that financial education is deliberately excluded from school curricula. Instead, we are taught how to work for money and become employees. Television and advertising then influence our spending habits. But where does financial education fit into this equation? Who teaches us how to manage money and make it work for us? Money should be our employee, just as it is mine, and it should be yours, too.

Universities often rely on funding from large corporations or wealthy families. Consequently, when students complete their studies, these entities offer them guaranteed jobs. This situation may seem appealing at first, but I propose that these companies and families view universities as nothing more than recruitment centers. They seek out the brightest individuals to become their employees, who will generate massive amounts of passive income for themselves. If this strategy is deemed suitable for them, shouldn't it be suitable for us as well? Therefore, we must prioritize our financial education.

Many of my friends believe that acquiring additional degrees will directly correlate with their earning potential. To some degree, there is some truth to this, but it never results in the financial freedom that they aspire to achieve. However, I encourage you to investigate for yourselves the fact that some of the most successful people in the world are university dropouts. It is amusing to witness individuals like Warren Buffett receiving honorary degrees from prestigious institutions despite never having attended them.

In fact, Buffett attempted to gain admission to Harvard but was rejected. Yet, due to his remarkable success, he was bestowed with an honorary degree. Similarly, Michael Dell, the founder of Dell Computers, is also a university dropout. It demonstrates that a university degree is not, although important, a prerequisite for achieving wealth. What truly matters is financial education.

To attain financial education, I would advise you to take a proactive approach. This situation can be achieved by reading books, listening to educational podcasts, attending seminars, or joining cash flow clubs where like-minded individuals discuss and explore financial matters. **This is the truth about becoming wealthy – it lies in your financial education.** I commend you for acquiring this book, as its purpose is to initiate your financial education journey.

Today, money favors those who can effectively manage it and take care of it. Those who lack money management skills will always find themselves in a perpetual cycle of financial inadequacy, regardless of their income or number of jobs. You may have experienced this firsthand, starting with a modest, sufficient paycheck, only to find that it never quite satisfies your needs, even with subsequent raises. The issue does not lie in the amount of money you earn but instead in your ability to manage your resources. Consequently, money tends to avoid those who lack financial intelligence. By purchasing this book, you have taken the first step in enhancing your financial IQ.

STEP 3
KNOWING THE HISTORY OF MONEY

Let's delve into the fascinating history of money and its evolution. Money is a medium of exchange that facilitates transactions and represents value. In ancient times, gold, silver, and other precious metals were widely used as money. However, carrying large amounts of gold and silver around became impractical for everyday transactions, not to mention not safe.

To overcome this challenge, the concept of representative money emerged. Instead of physically exchanging gold, people started using paper notes representing a specific amount of gold or silver. This system prevailed until 1971 and was known as the gold standard. Under the gold standard, countries held a certain amount of gold reserves, and their currencies were pegged to the value of gold in possession of the country. For instance, if the United States had 1000 ounces of gold, they could print $35 for each ounce, totaling $35,000.

However, the gold standard faced a significant problem during President Nixon's reign. As Americans began purchasing cheaper products from Asia, the country's wealth started flowing outwards. To address this, President Nixon abandoned the gold standard and introduced fiat currency. This type of currency is not backed by a physical commodity like gold but is instead based on trust in the issuing government. It means that money is no longer inherently valuable but derives its worth from the belief that it can be exchanged for goods and services.

One consequence of this shift is that fiat currency tends to devalue over time. For example, in 1969, when my mother-in-law was 30 years old, one ounce of gold was US$35. As of the day of writing, 28th May 2024, an ounce of gold is now US$2,357.52. It has increased by 6,735 percent since 1969. This apparent increase in value is actually a result of the depreciation of the currency rather than the intrinsic worth of the asset (the gold).

With all of that said, today, the gold that backed that $35,000 of currency might not even be there anymore. So we print and print, and then we print some more. With very little to no constraint, we put our faith in the issuing government that their fiat currency will stand the test of time as gold has for thousands of years. I'm afraid I'm lacking in such faith.

This understanding leads to the realization that saving money in its traditional sense is not a wise long-term strategy. Fiat currency is designed to lose value over time, making savers the losers in this financial game. **When they speak about inflation, we are talking about the purchasing power of your "money." If inflation is at 7%, it means your money has lost 7% of its purchasing power from the previous year. The Financially Free are aware of this fact, so they focus on alternative methods of preserving and growing their wealth. By sharing this knowledge, I aim to make this secret public and help individuals avoid the pitfalls of relying solely on saving for retirement!**

YEAR	AMOUNT	INFLATION RATE	NEW VALUE
2018	$1,000.00	3.74%	$962.60
2019	$962.60	3.91%	$924.96
2020	$924.96	5.23%	$876.59
2021	$876.59	5.86%	$825.22
2022	$825.22	10.35%	$739.81
2023	$739.81	6.47%	$691.94
2024	$691.94	7%	$643.51

$1000 left in the bank for 6 years. New purchasing power is $643.51

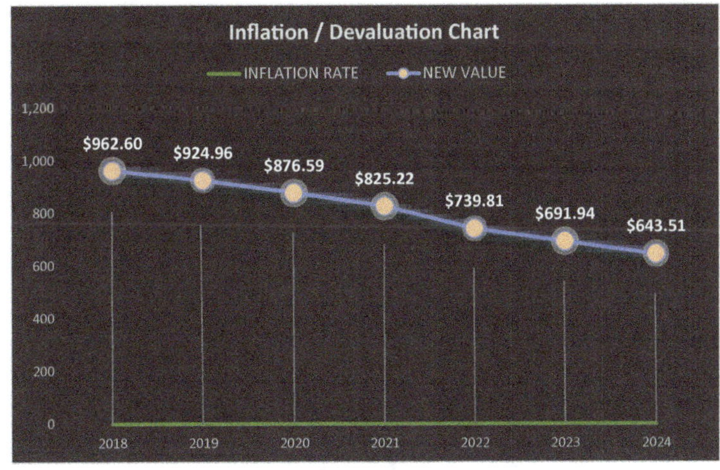

STEP 4

LEARN TO READ AND UNDERSTAND A FINANCIAL STATEMENT

In this chapter, we will explore the financial statement. It is a powerful tool that can empower you to take control of your financial life. A financial statement consists of four key components: the income box, where money flows in; the expense box, where money flows out; the asset box, which represents your valuable possessions; and the liabilities box, which includes your debts.

Additionally, there is a line on the right side known as the passive income line, which will be explained further. Understanding and utilizing these four boxes can potentially transform your financial situation for the better, as it did for me.

Notes

Financial Statement	Month (MM/YY): _____________	
Income		
Income # 1	$	
Income # 2	$	
	$	
	$	
	$	
Real Estate	$	
Other	$	
Total OTC		$
Other Income	$	
Total Income		$
Total Passive Income		$

Expenses		
Mortgage	$	
Food - Supermarket	$	
Food - Eating Out	$	
Liquor	$	
School Fees, Uniform Etc	$	
Phone & Internet	$	
Cable TV	$	
Life Insurance	$	
Electricity	$	
Water	$	
	$	
	$	
	$	
	$	
	$	
	$	
	$	
MISC	$	
Total Expenses		$

Notes

Assets		
Bank Accounts	$	
Cash In Hand	$	
		$
Business - Fair Market Value		
Business # 1	$	
Business # 2	$	
Business # 3	$	
		$
Others		
Cars	$	
Furniture	$	
		$
Total Assets		$

Liabilities		
Mortage	$	
Cars # 1	$	
Cars # 2	$	
Credit Card 1	$	
Credit Card 2	$	
Credit Card 3	$	
Loan # 1	$	
Loan # 2	$	
Total Liabilities		$

Total Net Worth	$

Notes

STEP 5
MANAGING YOUR EXPENSES

In our expense box, we have various items that we spend our hard-earned money on. It is crucial to have a clear understanding of our expenses and manage them effectively. Don't be afraid to take control and list your expenses, as, in many cases, they may not be as bad as you imagine. Unfortunately, many people do not budget and end up spending more than they earn, which can lead to financial difficulties.

Personal Monthly Budget

INCOME	Projected	Actual	Difference
Wages			
Tips			
Interest			
Dividends			
Gifts Received			
Other			
Total Income	$	$	$

Home Expenses	Projected	Actual	Difference
Mortgage/Rent			
Electricity			
Water			
Home Phone			
Mobile Phone(credit)			
School Fees/Uniform			
Lunch Money			
Credit Card Payments			
Gas			
Insurance			
Cable/Satellite			
Internet			
Furnishings/Appliances			
Food			
Hair			
Nails			
Clothes			
Entertainment			
Car Payments			
Car Insurance			
Car Rego			
Taxi Fare			
Eduactional Material			
Other			
Total Expenses	$	$	$

Total Expenses	$	$	$

Some usual monthly expenses include petrol, day-care fees, and rent. It is essential to take control of your expense box by deciding where your money goes, when it is spent, and how much is allocated to each expense. This level of management allows you to make informed decisions about your spending habits.

I want to address my fellow Jamaicans specifically when it comes to the allure of material possessions and the desire for bling. It is essential to recognize that spending excessive amounts of money on fashion items that quickly become outdated is not a wise use of our resources. Instead, consider redirecting that money towards more valuable investments, such as books, courses, or seminars that can enhance your financial IQ, knowledge, and skills. The more you increase your financial IQ, the more money will flow in your direction! Financial Education is a powerful tool for personal growth and financial success.

Investing in yourself is a wise expense. Once you have made investments that generate income, saving the money earned from those investments is advisable. Accumulate your savings until you have enough to make further investments. Avoid leaving your money in the bank for too long, as the interest rates they offer are often lower than they charge for loans. Take note of the difference in treatment when you visit the bank.

People standing in line are depositing their money, while those borrowing money are given personalized attention in a comfortable setting.

This practice indicates that simply saving money is not a fruitful strategy, and spending money unwisely is even worse.

It is crucial to educate ourselves about the financial institutions and businesses we interact with. Banks and car dealerships are profit-driven entities, and their advertisements often encourage immediate gratification through buying new cars and houses.

	CAR LOAN PER MILLION$	10%			3%			
YEAR	AMOUNT TO PURCHASE CAR	DEPOSIT PAID	LOAN AMOUNT	INTEREST RATE	ADDITIONAL FEES	INTERST PAID YEARLY		VALUE OF CAR
1	$ 1,000,000.00	$ 100,000.00	$ 900,000.00	15%	$ 27,000.00	$ 135,000.00		$1,000,000.00
2						$ 128,350.97		$ 900,000.00
3						$ 120,704.59		$ 810,000.00
4						$ 111,911.25		$ 729,000.00
5						$ 101,798.91		$ 656,100.00
6						$ 90,169.72		$ 590,490.00
7						$ 76,796.14		$ 531,441.00
8						$ 61,416.54		$ 489,296.90
9						$ 43,729.99		$ 430,467.21
10						$ 23,390.46		$ 387,420.49
		$ 100,000.00	$ 900,000.00		$ 27,000.00	$ 893,268.57		
								CAR VALUE IN 10 YEARS
		TOTAL PER MILLION DOLLARS BORROWED OVER A 10 YEAR PERIOD					$1,920,268.57	$ 387,420.49

However, it is important to delay this gratification and focus on building your financial stability and knowledge. The time will come when you can afford these luxuries, but it is essential to make informed decisions and prioritize long-term financial well-being.

Speaking of houses, it is a common misconception that a house is always an asset. While a property can be considered an asset, it is important to understand the full picture. In the context of a bank's balance sheet, your house is listed as an asset for the bank, but it is a liability for you as the homeowner. We will explore this concept further in the discussion of the financial statement.

Congratulations again for reaching this far in the book.

In summary, take control of your:

1.	expenses,
2.	budgeting wisely
3.	investing in your education
4.	and future

These are key steps to achieving financial success. It is crucial to understand the nature of financial institutions and make informed decisions that align with your long-term goals.

Notes

STEP 6
INCOME

When it comes to income, there are distinctions between good income and bad income. Good income refers to passive income, which continues to flow even when you are not actively working for it. This type of income provides you with the freedom to spend your time as you wish – without being tied to a traditional job. Passive income streams are created by investing your money and allowing it to work for you.

On the other hand, bad income refers to income that requires you to exchange most of your time for money. This type of income is limited by the number of hours in a day and the amount of energy you have. Working multiple jobs to make ends meet can lead to exhaustion and strain on personal relationships.

Passive Income

It is important to create passive income streams to achieve financial success. It involves using the money you earn from your primary sources of income to invest in assets that generate ongoing income. That is your job! You must convert your earned income to passive income. One effective way to build wealth is by investing in real estate. Real estate offers the advantage of leverage, allowing you to use a smaller amount of your own money to secure financing for a property. Additionally, real estate ownership provides the potential for capital gains as the value of the property appreciates over time.

Investing in real estate requires education and careful decision-making. It is advisable to read books, watch videos, find mentors, and build a team of professionals to guide you through the process, and no, it won't be free. Mistakes may be made along the way, but they present opportunities for learning and growth. Ultimately, success in real estate investing comes from minimizing mistakes and maximizing profits.

Managed funds, on the other hand, may not be a preferred option for passive income. While some individuals find success with managed funds, others prefer to have more control over their investments, and if you do decide to invest in managed funds, please make sure the fees are affordable. Fees as little as 2% can be a killer on your returns over time. Investing in savings accounts offered by banks may provide some passive income, but the returns are often low compared to other investment opportunities.

Another avenue for generating passive income is through owning and running businesses. Building a successful business can lead to significant financial gains. However, it is important to recognize that managing a business can be more challenging than investing in real estate. The key to success in business is building a strong team of individuals who can contribute their skills and expertise. Being the smartest person on your team is not advisable! For starters, when building your business, you need less money and more sweat equity.

In summary, creating passive income streams is essential for achieving financial freedom. Investing in real estate, businesses, and other income-generating assets allows your money to work for you, not sitting in an air-conditioned bank while you toil in the hot sun! Educating yourself, making informed investment decisions, and building a team of professionals to support your financial goals is crucial. Remember, the costliest advice is free advice.

Before we move on to the next segment, let's take a moment to discuss the concept of passive income and liabilities.

Passive income refers to income that continues to flow even when you are not actively working. It allows you to spend your time as you wish without being tied to a traditional job. Passive income streams are created by investing your money and allowing it to work for you. This can be achieved through various investment vehicles, such as real estate, businesses, and managed funds.

STEP 7
LIABILITIES

It is essential to differentiate between good debt and bad debt when it comes to liabilities. Good debt is the type that makes you money, such as borrowing money to invest in income-generating assets. On the other hand, bad debt is the type that costs you money, such as borrowing money for personal expenses, carnival, buying a car on loan, and purchasing a home that is too expensive for your financial situation, just for you to live in.

Owning a home is often seen as a rite of passage, but it can be a liability if it is not generating income for you. Renting out your home and receiving positive cash flow can turn it into an asset. Similarly, a car is typically seen as a liability. However, if you use it for income-generating purposes, such as a taxi or a tour bus, it can become an asset.

When considering liabilities and assets, educating yourself and learning to read the numbers is essential. Understand which debts to avoid and which investments have the potential to generate positive cash flow. This knowledge can significantly improve your financial position.

Lastly, it is essential to redefine the concept of assets. An asset should be anything that puts money in your pocket rather than something that takes money out. This definition differs from what traditional banks may consider assets, such as a house or furniture.

By understanding the principles of passive income and liabilities and redefining assets, you can make more informed financial decisions and work towards achieving financial freedom.

Notes

STEP 8
ASSETS

Let's further discuss the concept of assets and liabilities. You are correct in stating that some things traditionally considered assets may not align with the "true" definition of an asset, which is something that puts money in your pocket. For example, when you take a loan to purchase furniture, the furniture becomes the bank's/ store's asset because it is putting money in their pocket through interest payments. In contrast, it becomes a liability for you because it takes money out of your pocket.

Similarly, your house is not considered an asset unless you are renting it out, Airbnb included, and generating positive cash flow. The same applies to your car, which is typically seen as a liability but can become an asset if used for income-generating purposes like a taxi or paid tours.

Notes

STEP 9
READING THE NUMBERS

It is essential to learn to read the numbers and understand where things truly stand in your financial statement to increase your financial IQ. Educating yourself about the difference between good and bad expenses, liabilities, and assets will enable you to make informed financial decisions.

Now, let's discuss how the different components of a financial statement relate to each other. A poor person's financial statement typically consists of income from a job, which goes into the income box and then directly to the expense box. It results in no savings or investments, leading to a lack of passive income.

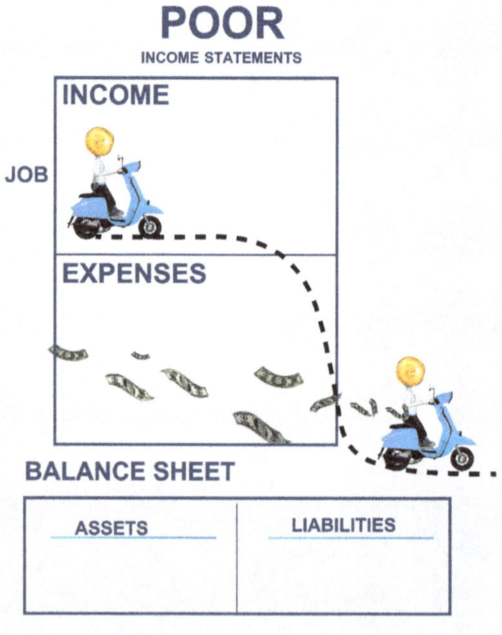

On the other hand, a middle-class financial statement starts with income from a job, which goes into the income box. However, it travels down to the liabilities box instead of the expense box. This is because the middle class often spends their income on liabilities, such as the house they live in or luxury items like sports cars and boats. The income is then used to make monthly payments on these liabilities.

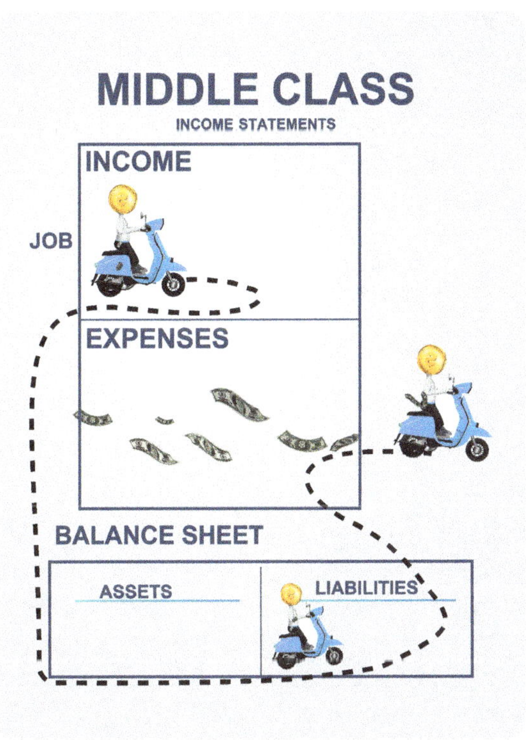

In contrast, a rich person's financial statement looks different. Their income is not derived solely from a job but rather from the asset column. They create businesses or invest in income-generating assets, and the income from these assets flows into the income box. The financially free people focus on accumulating assets that generate more income, enabling them to create additional assets and continue the cycle.

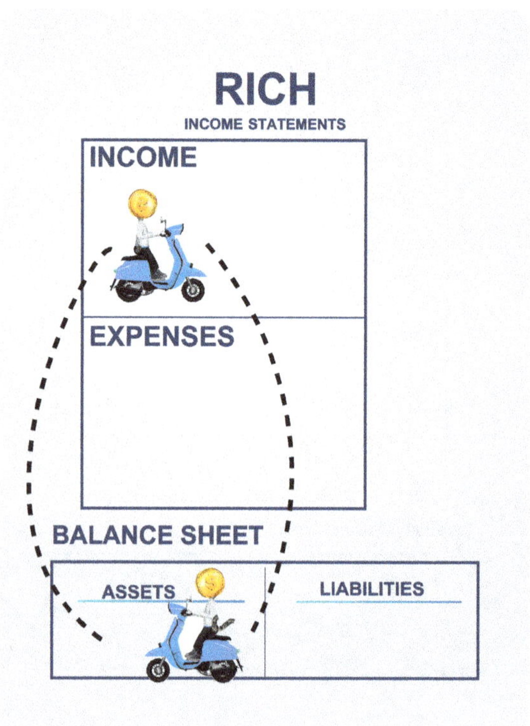

The goal is to reach a point where the income from your assets surpasses your monthly expenses. At that point, you have the option to retire and dedicate your time to creating more businesses and assets. We should be getting wealthier as we get older! It's important to note that experiencing temporary financial setbacks or losses does not make someone poor. Financially Free individuals may encounter losses when investing or starting businesses, but they view these experiences as valuable lessons that make them smarter for future endeavors. Being broke is a temporary state while being poor is a long-term condition perpetuated by a lack of financial knowledge and the cycle of generational poverty. Poverty starts in the mind, not the pocket!

It is crucial to focus on creating assets that generate income to break free from this cycle. I believe every "toy" you have, boat, car, or home, should be supported by a business or asset that generates enough resources to cover its costs. Your hard-earned income should not be wasted. That earned income needs to be converted into a passive income stream in time, but if it's all gone, there you have it! A lost opportunity!

In conclusion, by understanding the true definition of an asset, anything that puts money in your pocket, and liabilities, anything that takes money from your pocket, and learning to read the numbers in your financial statement, you can make smarter financial decisions and work towards building a solid foundation of assets that generate passive income. Keep reading, and I will show you how to read those numbers.

<u>ROBERT KYOSAKI'S CASHFLOW QUADRANT</u>

In Robert Kiyosaki's Cashflow Quadrant, there are four categories represented by different letters. On the left side of the quadrant, there are two Es and an Ss. The Es represent employees, while the S represents small business owners or self-employed individuals. These individuals often have specialized skills and are considered the "smart people" in their respective fields.

On the right side of the quadrant, there are 'Bs' and 'Is'. The 'Bs' represent big business owners or entrepreneurs, while the 'Is' represent investors. These individuals speak a different language and have different priorities than employees and small business owners.

Employees and small business owners are focused on benefits and job security. They may prioritize factors like dental and medical benefits. On the other hand, big business owners and investors are more concerned with returns on investment and when they will receive their money back. It's important to note that individuals can fall into multiple categories in the Cashflow Quadrant. For example, someone can be an employee and an investor simultaneously. However, the goal is to move towards the right side of the quadrant, particularly towards being an investor (I). Investors aim to have their money work for them and generate passive income.

Robert Kiyosaki also developed a board game called Cashflow, which aims to teach players how to convert their earned income into passive income. I strongly recommend you buy a copy. The objective is to reach a point where passive income exceeds monthly expenses, allowing individuals to escape the "rat race" and enter the "fast track" of wealth generation. Fast track is characterized by generating significant income and having more time and freedom.

Wealth is not solely measured by the number of zeros in one's bank account but also by how long one can sustain one's desired lifestyle without actively working. The concept of old money versus new money refers to those who have figured out that wealth is measured in time and have created generational wealth.

FINANCIAL IQ

Understanding key financial terms such as assets, liabilities, leverage, cash flow, good debt, bad debt, and return on investment (ROI) is crucial to increase one's financial IQ. Learning and using the appropriate language and context for these terms is essential for making smart financial decisions.

Increasing financial education and taking control of one's financial future are emphasized to build wealth and live the desired lifestyle. Educating oneself through books, mentorship, seminars, and discussions with like-minded individuals is recommended.

The goal is to focus on the asset column, increase your passive income, and achieve financial freedom. By minding one's own business, the business of your life, and focusing on your personal wealth creation rather than solely enriching others, we can take control of our financial destiny.

Continuing one's financial education and proactively managing finances is crucial for long-term success and wealth accumulation.

Doctors use the language of doctors, and lawyers use the language of lawyers. To improve your financial education, here are a few commonly used words in the financial world:

DEFINITIONS

Here is an extensive list of commonly used terms in financial education materials:

A: <u>Asset</u> – Something of value that is owned by an individual, organization, or company. But for the purposes of this book, an Asset is anything that puts money in your pocket.

<u>Amortization</u> – The process of gradually paying off a debt or loan over a period through regular payments.

<u>Annual Percentage Rate (APR)</u> – The annualized interest rate that includes both the interest and fees associated with a loan or credit card.

B: <u>Budget</u> – A plan that outlines income and expenses to manage finances effectively.

<u>Bonds</u> – Debt securities that are issued by governments or corporations to raise capital. Bondholders receive regular interest payments and the principal amount at maturity.

<u>Bear Market</u> – A market condition characterized by falling prices and pessimistic investor sentiment.

<u>Balance Sheet</u> – A financial statement that provides a snapshot of a company's assets, liabilities, and shareholders' equity at a specific point in time.

C: <u>Capital</u> – Financial resources, such as money or assets, that are used to generate income or investment returns.

<u>Credit Score</u> – A numerical representation of an individual's credit worthiness, based on their credit history and financial behavior.

<u>Cash Flow</u> – The net amount of cash and cash equivalents that flow in and out of a business over a specific period.

<u>Compound Interest</u> – Interest that is calculated on both the initial principal and the accumulated interest from previous periods.

D: <u>Debt</u> – Money owed to another party, typically with the expectation of repayment.

<u>Dividend</u> – A portion of a company's earnings that is distributed to its shareholders on a per-share basis.

<u>Derivative</u> – A financial contract whose value is derived from an underlying asset, such as stocks, bonds, or commodities.

<u>Debt-to-Equity Ratio</u> – A financial ratio that compares a company's total debt to its shareholders' equity, indicating the proportion of financing provided by debt versus equity.

<u>Diversification</u> – Diversification is the strategy of spreading investments across different assets or asset classes to reduce risk. By diversifying, investors can mitigate the impact of any single investment's poor performance on their overall portfolio.

E: <u>Equity</u> – The value of an asset after deducting any liabilities or debts associated with it.

<u>Exchange-Traded Fund (ETF)</u> – A type of investment fund that trades on stock exchanges, representing a basket of securities.

<u>Expense Ratio</u> – The percentage of a mutual fund's assets that are used to cover operating expenses.

F: <u>Financial Independence</u> – The ability to meet all financial obligations and maintain a desired lifestyle without relying on external sources of income.

<u>Financial Statement</u> – A financial statement is a formal record of a company's financial activities, such as its income, expenses, assets, and liabilities. The three main types of financial statements are the balance sheet, income statement, and cash flow statement.

<u>Fixed Income</u> – Fixed income refers to investments that provide a fixed or regular income stream. It includes bonds, certificates of deposit (CDs), and other debt securities issued by governments, corporations, or financial institutions.

G: <u>Gross Income</u> – The total income earned before any deductions or taxes.

<u>Gross Domestic Product (GDP)</u> – GDP measures a country's economic output. It represents the total value of all goods and services produced within a country's borders in a specific time period. GDP is often used to gauge the overall health and growth of an economy.

<u>Growth Stock</u> – A growth stock is a type of stock issued by a company that is expected to grow at an above-average rate compared to other companies in the market. Investors are attracted to growth stocks for their potential for capital appreciation.

H: <u>Hedge Fund</u> – A hedge fund is an investment fund that pools capital from accredited individuals or institutional investors to invest in various assets. Hedge funds are known for using alternative investment strategies, such as short selling, derivatives, and leverage, to generate returns.

<u>Holding Period</u> – Holding period refers to the length of time an investor holds an investment before selling it. It is an important factor in determining the tax implications of an investment, as long-term holdings may qualify for lower tax rates.

I: <u>Inflation</u> – The rate at which the general level of prices for goods and services is rising, resulting in a decrease in purchasing power.

<u>Investment</u> – The act of allocating money or resources to an asset or venture with the expectation of generating income or profit.

<u>Index Fund</u> – An index fund is a type of mutual fund or exchange-traded fund (ETF) that aims to replicate the performance of a specific market index, such as the S&P 500. Index funds are known for their low costs and passive investment approach.

J: <u>Joint Account</u> – A joint account is a bank or investment account that two or more individuals share. Each account holder has equal access to the funds and can make transactions on behalf of the account.

<u>Junk Bond</u> – A junk bond, also known as a high-yield bond, is a bond issued by a company or government entity with a lower credit rating than

investment-grade bonds. Junk bonds offer higher yields to compensate for the higher risk of default.

K: <u>Key Performance Indicator (KPI)</u> – A key performance indicator is a measurable metric used to evaluate the success or performance of an organization, project, or individual. KPIs are often specific to the goals and objectives of the entity being measured.

<u>KYC (Know Your Customer)</u> – KYC is a process implemented by financial institutions to verify the identity and assess the suitability of their customers. It involves collecting and verifying customer information to prevent money laundering, fraud, and other illegal activities.

L: <u>Liquidity</u> – The ease with which an asset or investment can be converted into cash without affecting its market price.

<u>Leverage</u> – Leverage refers to the use of borrowed funds to increase the potential return on an investment. It involves using debt to finance an investment with the expectation that the returns will exceed the cost of borrowing. However, leverage also amplifies potential losses.

M: <u>Mortgage</u> – A loan used to finance the purchase of real estate, typically with specified repayment terms and interest rates.

<u>Mutual Fund</u> – A mutual fund is a type of investment vehicle that pools money from multiple investors to invest in a diversified portfolio of securities, such as stocks, bonds, or other assets. Mutual funds are managed by professional fund managers.

<u>Market Capitalization</u> – Market capitalization, often referred to as a market cap, is the total value of a company's outstanding shares of stock. It is calculated by multiplying the current share price by the total number of shares outstanding. Market cap is used to classify companies as large-cap, mid-cap, or small-cap.

N: <u>Net Worth</u> – The value of an individual's assets minus their liabilities, representing their overall financial position.

<u>Net Income</u> – Net income, also known as net profit or net earnings, is the

amount of money a company has left over after deducting all expenses, taxes, and interest from its total revenue. It is a measure of a company's profitability.

NASDAQ – NASDAQ is a global electronic marketplace for buying and selling securities. It is the second-largest stock exchange in the world by market capitalization and is known for listing many technology and growth-oriented companies.

O: Over-the-Counter (OTC) – Refers to the trading of financial instruments directly between parties outside of a centralized exchange.

Operating Income – The profit generated from a company's core business operations, calculated by subtracting operating expenses from revenue.

Opportunity Cost – The potential benefit that is sacrificed when choosing one option over another.

P: Price-Earnings Ratio (P/E Ratio) – A valuation metric that measures the relative value of a company's stock by dividing its market price per share by its earnings per share.

Principal – The original amount of money invested or borrowed, excluding any interest or returns.

Portfolio – A collection of financial investments, such as stocks, bonds, or mutual funds, held by an individual or organization.

Q: Qualified Retirement Plan – A tax-advantaged retirement savings plan that meets specific requirements set by the Internal Revenue Service (IRS), such as 401(k) or IRA.

R: Return on Investment (ROI) – A measure of the profitability or efficiency of an investment, calculated by dividing the net profit by the initial investment and expressing it as a percentage.

Risk Management - The process of identifying, assessing, and prioritizing risks to minimize potential losses and protect assets.

Retirement - The period in a person's life when they stop working and rely on accumulated savings or investments for income.

S: <u>Stock Market</u> – A marketplace where shares of publicly traded companies are bought and sold.

<u>Securities</u> – Financial instruments, such as stocks, bonds, or options, that represent ownership or debt obligations.

T: <u>Taxes</u> – Mandatory financial contributions imposed by the government on individuals and businesses to fund public services and programs.

<u>Trade Surplus</u> – A favorable economic condition where the value of a country's exports exceeds the value of its imports.

<u>Treasury Bills (T-Bills)</u> – Short-term debt securities issued by the government with a maturity period of one year or less.

U: <u>Underlying Asset</u> – The financial asset or security on which a derivative contract is based, such as a stock, commodity, or index.

<u>Unit Trust</u> – A collective investment scheme where investors pool their money to invest in a diversified portfolio of assets.

V: <u>Volatility</u> – A statistical measure of the fluctuations or variability of the price of a financial instrument over time, indicating its risk or uncertainty.

<u>Value at Risk (VaR)</u> – A risk management metric that estimates the maximum potential loss of an investment or portfolio within a specific level of confidence.

W: <u>Wealth</u> – The accumulation of valuable assets, financial resources, and investments over time.

<u>Working Capital</u> – The measure of a company's short-term financial health, calculated by subtracting current liabilities from current assets.

<u>Write-off</u> – The accounting practice of removing an asset or liability from the books as a loss or expense.

X: <u>X-axis</u> – In financial charts and graphs, the horizontal line that represents the passage of time or different categories.

Y: <u>Yield Curve</u> - A graphical representation of the yields on bonds with different maturities, indicating the relationship between interest rates and time to maturity.

Z: <u>Zero-sum Game</u> - A situation in which one participant's gain is exactly offset by another participant's loss, resulting in a net balance of zero.

Note: Please note that this is not an exhaustive list, but it includes some of the most used terms in finance.

ANSELS PREFERRED READING LIST

- ▶ "7 Habits of Highly Effective People" by Stephen R. Covey
- ▶ "Who moved my Cheese" by Spencer Johnson M.D.
- ▶ "Cash Flow Quadrant" by Robert T. Kiyosaki
- ▶ "The Power of Habit" by Charles Duhigg
- ▶ "Unshakeable: Your Financial Freedom Playbook" by Tony Robbins
- ▶ "The Millionaire Next Door" by Thomas J. Stanley
- ▶ "The Millionaire Mind" by Thomas J. Stanley
- ▶ "Money/master the Game" by Tony Robbins
- ▶ "Smarter Faster Better" by Charles Duhigg
- ▶ "Good to Great" by James C. Collins
- ▶ "The naked CEO" by Alex Malley
- ▶ "Invest like a Bank" by Beaux Blast
- ▶ "The Psychology of Money" by Morgan Housel
- ▶ "The subtle art of Not giving a F*ck" by Mark Manson
- ▶ "Built to last" by James C. Collins and Jerry I. Porras
- ▶ "Walk Away Wealthy" by Mark Tepper